Alfred Nobel

Betty Lou Kratoville

High Noon Books

ORDER DIRECTLY FROM
ANN ARBOR PUBLISHERS LTD.
P.O. BOX 1, BELFORD
NORTHUMBERLAND NE70 7JX
TEL. 01668 214460 FAX 01668 214484
www.annarbor.co.uk

International Standard Book Number: 1-57128-231-9

10 09 08 07 06 05 04 03 02 01
0 9 8 7 6 5 4 3 2 1

You'll enjoy all the High Noon Books. Write for
our catalog that lists and describes titles.

Contents

Chapter 1

Early Years

The place was a back room on the second floor of a shabby apartment building in Stockholm, Sweden. The time was October 21, 1833. The event was the birth of Alfred Bernhard Nobel.

The baby was so small, so weak, it could barely cry. His mother, Caroline, wept as she held the tiny infant in her arms. Somehow, she vowed, she would nurse him to health. She knew the rest of the family had given up hope. Not Caroline!

For eight years Caroline Nobel kept careful watch over her frail third son. It was never easy. The baby had a weak spine so it was years before he could sit up alone. He often had an upset stomach. Now and then it was hard for him to breathe. But his mother never gave up. And by the time Alfred was eight, although he was never strong, she no longer had to lie awake nights worrying.

Later in his life, Alfred often wondered how his mother had gone on day after day. The family was poor. Alfred's father was a brilliant man. But, as is so often the case, he was not a good businessman. The rooms the family lived in were swept by icy winter drafts. A single stove gave out a bit of heat but never enough. Light came from smoky oil lamps that made Alfred and his brothers cough and wipe runny eyes and noses. Food was scarce. Dried codfish was served at every meal and not much else. Garbage was tossed into a corner of the back yard. It drew packs of bold, hungry rats.

In these years, Stockholm had thousands and thousands of pitifully poor people. Epidemics swept through the city. Almost every family lost at least one child to whooping cough or measles or other disease.

Many men were out of work. Among these

was Alfred's father. Immanuel Nobel spent his days puttering with inventions. They either did not work or did not sell. His mother, on the other hand, rose before dawn. She cleaned, she patched, she cooked the skimpy meals. Somehow she held the family together. Sometimes Alfred's brothers sold matches on a Stockholm street corner to help their mother.

Out of all this misery, Alfred had one happy memory. It was Christmas Eve. Caroline managed to see that her boys did not miss the jolly Swedish customs. They gulped *dipp i grytan* (bread dipped in a special broth). They danced around the small Christmas tree. They sang "Silent Night." Alfred never forgot these childhood Christmases. They were spots of beauty and color in a bleak childhood.

When Alfred was four, his father left the family behind in Sweden. He went to Russia to seek work. Caroline had no idea how she would support herself and her sons. It did not take her long to come up with a plan.

She borrowed money from family and

friends. Then she opened a small store. In it she sold milk, butter, cheese, and a few vegetables. The poor woman worked from dawn to late at night. But in time the store began to show a small profit. Now she could think about sending her sons to school.

Eldest son Robert was the first to be enrolled in the Jacob Parish School. Next came Ludwig. Then, when he was seven, it was Alfred's turn. Jacob Parish was a school for poor children. It was a gloomy, cruel place. Boys were beaten every day. Six spelling mistakes was a crime. The poor student was commanded to come to the teacher's desk at the front of the room. Ten trembling fingers were placed on its edge. Smash! Down came six painful lashes!

Alfred was luckier than most boys. First of all, his mother had already taught him to read and spell. Next, he had his father's brilliant mind. Last, he was willing to work hard. He quickly became a model student. His grades were high. No beatings for Alfred!

In the meantime, Immanuel was doing quite well in Russia. He had found a job at last. He built sea and land mines for the army. In 1842, when Alfred was nine, Immanuel had saved enough money to send for his family. Passports were given for "Mrs. Nobel and children, all minors."

It was a shabby group that left Sweden in their mended clothes. Caroline was nearing 30. She was still a handsome woman with clear blue eyes and masses of dark gold hair. Her sons adored her. But she was tired. The years without her husband had been hard. Her sons had come to her with all their problems.

By the time they were ready to leave, Caroline had taught the three boys a few Russian words. Alfred soon taught himself other words that he would need in the new country. After only a year in Russia, he could speak its language easily and well.

The family traveled first by ship and then by coach. The roads were rough. The trip in the overcrowded damp coach seemed to take forever. But Immanuel was waiting for them with a horse and a carriage and his own coachman. How surprised Caroline and the boys must have been to see Immanuel in fine clothes!

They soon learned that his inventions had been a success in this new country. He had strong contacts with the army and with the government. He was a changed man!

The Nobel's new home was a simple one-story wooden house on a canal. But it was far better than their apartment in Stockholm. Even so, poor Alfred suffered as much from cold and drafty rooms in St. Petersburg as he ever had in Sweden. But the Nobel family's way of life was much more comfortable. During this easy period, three more Nobel children were born. Only one son, Emil, survived. Alfred was to say later that Russia became almost a second homeland to the Nobel family.

Chapter 2

The Father and Three Sons

All three of the Nobel sons were sent to a school in St. Petersburg. Alfred did not last long. His spine was simply too weak to allow him to sit at a desk all day. By this time Immanuel Nobel was well known and growing rich. He was able to hire fine tutors for his sons. Alfred had a favorite tutor, Ivan Peterov. With this skilled man's help, Alfred quickly reached and passed his older brothers in all subjects. When he met with Peterov each morning, Alfred never knew what topic the lesson might cover – politics, history, science. It was not a formal education. Yet it could not have been a better one.

Alfred's nimble brain excelled at almost

any subject. He was amazingly gifted in foreign languages. As he grew older, he mastered Swedish, Russian, French, English, and German. He often wrote poetry in one or more of these languages. His father did not approve of his son becoming what Immanuel called a "pen man." He did all he could to discourage Alfred's writing.

When Alfred turned 16, his father offered him a chance to travel in other countries. There was only one catch. No more poetry writing! In fact, no writing of any kind. Alfred thought it over. Then he gave in. But he paid a price. He had a deep unfilled longing to write for the rest of his life. And he never stopped reading English poetry.

Alfred traveled first to Central Europe and then to England. Although very young, he was already a trained chemist. On this trip, he met with many of his father's business connections. They were deeply impressed with this sharp young chemist. They let him carry on his work in their labs.

One day, Alfred sailed for the United States. He was eager to meet John Ericcson, a fellow Swede. Ericcson was working on a number of inventions. The warm air engine he was working on interested Immanuel Nobel so he sent his son to find out about it. Alfred's letters home at this time are unclear. They seem to show that John and Alfred never became close friends although they did have great respect for one another's work.

It became time for Alfred to return to Russia and go to work for his father. He had picked up a lot of new ideas on his travels. He wanted to see which of them might have value in one or more of his father's many activities.

It may be that he drove himself too hard. His father's factories now employed more than a thousand men. The Crimean War was in full force. Workers put in extra hours and days. Alfred often stayed at his post in the lab all night. By the following summer he was weak and ill. The doctors felt the cause was overwork. Alfred was sent to a health spa. He called it the "bath and guzzle cure." After a few months he seemed well enough to leave the spa. He made a few stops at labs on the way home. But he was eager to get back to work.

Life and work for the Nobels were good as long as the Crimean War lasted. Then orders to their factories stopped. Profits also sank because the Russians did not pay their bills.

Immanuel tried to keep the factories going. He sent Alfred to borrow money from banks in Paris and London. They turned him down. The time had come for a change. The father and his three sons had a long meeting. It was decided that Immanuel would take his wife and youngest son, Emil, back to Stockholm. Robert, Ludwig, and Alfred would stay in Russia.

The three sons worked hard to save a small sum of money so that their father might start all over again in Sweden. It was difficult, but somehow they did it.

Ludwig married and got his own place. Robert and Alfred shared an apartment. Alfred soon turned the small kitchen into a lab. He began to get patents on inventions of his own. None of these early products with patents seem to have had lasting value. The brothers kept casting around for new ideas.

Then they heard of the work of a man named Sobrero. This man had discovered a new substance. He called it nitro-glycerin. Such a strange liquid! Such a *dangerous* liquid! It was heavy and oily and clear as water. When it blew up, as it often did, the gases it formed took up 10,000 times as much space as the liquid itself. There had to be a use for this powerful substance. But what could it be? The main problem was how to control it. Only then could it be used as an explosive. And, as usual, the world was trying for new ways to blow itself up!

Alfred and his brothers tried to solve the nitro-glycerin puzzle at their workshop in Russia. Immanuel tried to solve the puzzle at his workshop in Stockholm. The two groups did not always agree on the best method to do this. And that is where matters stood until the Heleneborg disaster!

Chapter 3

The Heleneborg Disaster

The time had come for Alfred to return to his own country. He knew his father needed help. Immanuel was an inventor. He was *not* a chemist. Yet he was working with nitro-glycerin. Alfred's two brothers decided to stay in Russia. They had started a small factory. They made machines and tools. This new business was showing a profit so they did not want to leave it.

Alfred was quite willing to go back to Sweden. He thought it might be easier to raise money for his own inventions there. Besides, he was eager to be with his mother and younger brother Emil again. Emil was now in college. He seemed to be just as brainy as his father and his brothers.

Some days Emil had free time from his college classes. Then he worked in his father's new lab at Heleneborg. Money was still tight so Nobel family members often helped out. At this time, Immanuel was excited about a recent breakthrough with controlling nitro-glycerin. Alfred did not agree with some of his father's findings. He knew that nitro-glycerin seldom reacted twice in the same way. He sensed danger. He warned his father about it. But the older man would not listen.

"After all," he said to his son, "I've been working with land mines and explosives for years. I know what I'm doing."

Little attention had been paid to some recent complaints. Neighbors nearby wondered about possible danger from work in the small lab. The landlord got in touch with the Nobels. They told him that the work going on in the lab was safe. They were terribly wrong.

September 3, 1864, was a beautiful fall day. Emil and three workers were busy at the rented

Heleneborg lab. Their task for that day was purifying glycerine.

A friend dropped in to watch Emil and his helpers fill an order from some railroad companies. The group chatted with the visitor as they worked. Suddenly the whole lab exploded with a thunderous roar. A huge yellow flame rose straight up in the air. Nearby buildings shook. Their windows shattered. People rushed from their homes into the streets. Had there been an earthquake?

Only small pieces and chunks were left of the lab. Everyone in it was killed. The Nobel family was crushed with grief and guilt. Nothing was worth the loss of their beloved Emil.

To make matters worse, no one seemed to know what had caused the terrible explosion. A trial was held. It shed little light on the tragedy. Five weeks later, Immanuel suffered a stroke. For a while he was paralyzed. After a few weeks he got back the use of his arms and legs and his speech. But he was never quite the same man again. His brain worked well enough. Yet his cheery outlook on life was gone forever.

Alfred blamed himself for the tragedy. Many years later when he had succeeded in making nitro-glycerin safe enough to be used, he would still mourn Emil. He would forever wish he could have come up with an answer sooner. It did not stop his willingness to tackle new problems. But he never forgot the dreadful day at Heleneborg.

Chapter 4

Carrying On

Alfred Nobel was not a man who gave up. It had been made clear that nitro-glycerine was useful. Orders for it poured in from all over the world. Yet, so did reports of terrible accidents caused by this strange liquid. Each accident sank Alfred into a deep depression. Each one made him think of Emil's death. Yet, he kept on with his work. Experiment followed experiment. He was sure that it was just a matter of mixing the nitro with another substance. Something spongy. Something harmless. Something that would soak up the nitro so that it could be shipped and used safely.

The answer, when it came, was almost by chance. One day Alfred put some stuff (cellulose nitrate) on a cut finger. He looked at it closely. Could this be mixed with nitro? He added a few drops of nitro to a mass of cellulose nitrate. The drops of nitro mixed easily with the cellulose nitrate. This was what he had been seeking! But there was still much work to be done.

Hour after hour he worked on a formula. How much nitro to how much cellulose nitrate? At last he came up with the right mixture. He gave the good news to his loyal aide. At once they began a series of 300 experiments. They had to be sure that what they had learned was safe before sharing it with the world. And this new material had to have a name. Alfred called it "dynamite."

What next? Work. A lot of work! A rough road with many bumps lay ahead for Alfred. First, a patent. He had worked too long and too hard to allow anyone else to produce dynamite. That meant he had to apply for a patent in every country where he hoped to build a factory. It sounded clearcut and simple. It was not.

Everywhere he turned there were lawsuits. There were men who claimed they had invented dynamite before Alfred. There were men who thought they could make minor changes in the formula. Then they could claim it as their own invention. All of these lawsuits cost a great deal of money. The stress also weakened Alfred's health, which had always worried his family and friends.

Luckily, there were also honest businessmen in the world. And there was a tremendous need for dynamite. It was used in blasting for roads, bridges, and buildings. Alfred was glad to grant licenses to manufacture dynamite to these honest men. They, in turn, paid him a sum of money for each stick of dynamite they made and sold. It helped pay the costs of some of the lawsuits.

What did dynamite look like? First of all, of course, it was no longer a liquid. It was now a solid tube – something like a large firecracker with a fuse at one end. It could be safely packed and shipped. It would not explode unless the

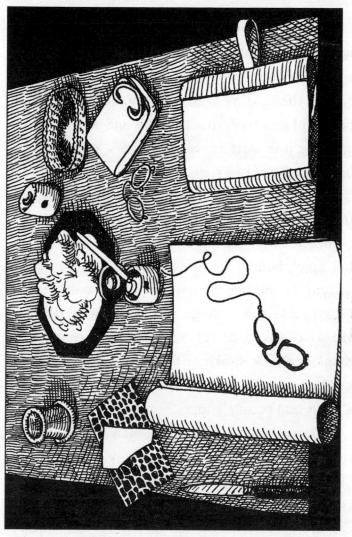

Nobel's desk

19

fuse was lit. It was a boon to mankind in the way it helped huge building projects all over the world. A boon to mankind? At first, Alfred Nobel thought yes. Surely dynamite was so powerful and so destructive, no one would think of using it in warfare. In later years, he found he had been terribly wrong.

Alfred hated to travel. And no wonder! In those days trains seldom ran on time. They were cold and dirty. Carriages on bumpy roads were not much better. Yet he was willing to travel to dozens of mining towns. There he could show how to use this strange new substance safely. He also wrote articles for newspapers and magazines. He spoke at town meetings. He did his best to calm worry and distrust. He did not always end people's fears.

It would take years for much of the world to accept dynamite. In this day and age of nuclear bombs, it is hard to understand how frightened people were of dynamite in the 19th century. But Alfred sensed their fears. He hoped that in time they would get over it.

Alfred put together a strong work force. He hired men who were honest and hardworking. He hired men who believed in the future of dynamite as strongly as he did.

By the late 1800s, he had opened factories in Sweden, Germany, Norway, Finland, Austria, England, and France. The whole world was becoming his marketplace. What about America?

Chapter 5

America

In 1866 Alfred decided it was time to see what he could do in America. Before he landed there in April, newspaper reports about his products were strongly negative. They wrote about accidents that were happening all over the world. They did not seem to understand that the fault did not lie with the new dynamite but with the liquid nitro. It was up to Alfred to explain this. He felt sure that he could do so.

One of the first things he did was ask to meet with the New York City mayor. He asked Mayor Hoffman to let him demonstrate his product. He wanted to show the American people, once and for all, that nitro, in its new form, would be risk-free for use in New York's many building projects. He also wrote a letter to the *New York Times*. In it he asked that no one make up his mind about dynamite until after the demonstration.

This took place in a quarry in upper New York City. Alfred showed onlookers that nitro alone did not explode unless it reached 360 degrees. It could therefore be safely used in making dynamite. A lot of people still did not believe him. He did hear from John Ericcson whom he had met in his 1850 trip to America. Ericcson gave him his full support.

During this visit Alfred set to work to get an American patent. It wasn't easy. Another group was seeking a patent for dynamite at the same time. To Alfred's great surprise, the court ruled in his favor even though he was not an American citizen.

Once the patent was granted, many men saw it as a way to quickly make a fortune. Companies were started. Factories were built. Few lasted. They were poorly managed. About this time Alfred heard that California gold miners were using the new explosive and calling it "giant powder." He then set up his own company. He named it the Giant Powder Company. He then took his American patent #57175 back to Germany. An American patent was important. After it was granted, letters and orders poured into his Hamburg office. Alfred never returned to the United States. He wrote to a friend:

Life in America was not pleasant to me in the long run. The stress over money destroys the many pleasures and ruins the sense of honor.

It was clear that Alfred had seen enough sharp businessmen and fortune hunters to last him a lifetime. Besides, he had much work to do.

Chapter 6

Man of Wealth

Alfred Nobel did not set out to become a rich man. Money was never important to him. Of course, he did not want to be poor again. But he had created something he felt would benefit the world. Now he had to be sure that those who needed it would be able to get it.

He started to look for good workers and foremen for his new factories. Crop failures had put a lot of men out of work all over Europe. They were happy to find jobs with Alfred. He was known for paying his workers well. He took good care of them and their families.

In only a few years factories all over the world were making dynamite. Profits soared. It was soon clear that the new explosive would be used in other ways than just peaceful ones. The Russian Czar was almost killed when a load of dynamite exploded under his dining room. A year later he did die when a dynamite-filled bomb blew up his carriage. Of course, Alfred heard of this. It depressed him deeply. This cruel use of dynamite would sadden him throughout his life.

He traveled much of the time. He never learned to enjoy it. He called trains his "rolling prisons." He did love to visit Paris. He thought highly of its people, its language, its arts. He bought a large house in Paris with a lab on the grounds. He grew orchids in his greenhouse. At first he gave large parties. Then he seemed to grow tired of them.

Letters begging for money came from all over the world. He now needed a staff to help him with this mail. He loved to tell the story about a staff member who was leaving to get married. Alfred asked the young woman what she wanted as a wedding present.

"Oh, just give me as much as *you* earn in

Nobel's home in Paris

one day," she replied quickly. Alfred was amused. He agreed without giving the matter much thought. And he kept his word even though he had to write her a check for $110,000!

He liked to stroll along the streets of Paris. He often stopped at a sidewalk cafe. He almost always dined alone at home or at a nearby restaurant.

Rich he might have been, yet he seemed a sad figure. At 40, he had begun to walk with a slight limp. His hair had turned gray. He had bushy eyebrows over blue, deep-set eyes. He wore a beard and usually dressed in a dark suit and white shirt.

Alfred was in constant pain from rheumatism. Now and then he had to go to bed with a migraine headache. It is no wonder that he was not always a cheerful man. About this time he said to a friend, "My life is dark and dismal."

Family and friends often wondered why he had never married. He hinted that marriage might hinder his ability to run the vast Nobel empire. His few friends did not agree but said nothing. But they felt sorry for this rich, unhappy man.

Alfred lived in Paris for 20 years. Then at age 60 he felt it was time for a change.

Chapter 7

The Brothers

While Alfred was building factories all over the world, his brothers were busy, too. Their work began when Robert Nobel decided to buy an oil field in Russia. He knew there were vast quantities of oil there. He had spent weeks walking across empty oil fields. He saw that very little drilling was going on.

At the time Robert had little money. He asked his brother Ludwig for a loan to buy the oil field. Ludwig gave him what he needed. This was common in the Nobel family. When one member needed help, another stepped up to give it.

Robert soon found that everything in the oil business was done in an old-fashioned way. Oil wells were dug by hand with shovels! Oil was stored in leather bags. It was taken to ports in carts. Robert knew he could do better than that. He also knew he needed help. He wrote Ludwig letter after letter. In each one he pleaded with Ludwig to come to the oil field. A few months later Ludwig got on a train and joined Robert. Soon they had several fields gushing oil.

Shipping oil to the coast in rickety carts would not do. The Nobels set to work and had a pipe line built to a port city. It was seven miles long. It was the first oil pipe line ever built in Russia. At the port, the oil was piped aboard huge tankers. These tankers were built for the Nobels in Sweden. It is often said that next to dynamite, the great tankers were the Nobels' most important gift to the world.

Oil was measured by a weight called a pood. Before the Nobels came, about 3,952,000 poods were taken from the wells each year in that part of Russia. After the Nobels, the amount soared to 123,500,000.

Years later, one day without warning

Robert did not show up for work. A month later he wrote that he had gone to a Swiss health spa to rest. It was thought that he might have tuberculosis. This was a common illness for workers in the oil fields in those days. At last he returned to his homeland, Sweden. Here he lived out his days with his family.

Now it was up to Ludwig to run the company. He did so for eight years. But he, too, caught a form of tuberculosis. He stuck it out as long as he could. Then his doctors insisted that he retire. He turned the firm over to his son and moved to a French town that was known for its healthy climate. He died there at the age of 57.

Chapter 8

Final Years

At this time Alfred had settled in a country home in San Remo in Southern Italy. It sat in the middle of a park with orange trees, beds of bright flowers, and a lovely view of the Mediterranean Sea. Alfred could not exist without a lab. He built one on the grounds of his new home. It had a machine shop, a chemical workroom, and a large library. A slim steel pier jutted out into the sea to be used for firing tests. Alfred called his new home "My Nest."

He spent most of his days in his lab. There seemed to be no end to his ideas. He worked on a substitute for rubber, on paints and varnishes, on new parts for telephones, batteries, and phonographs. He even tried to create rubies, sapphires, and other gems. No luck! Over the years he obtained more than 355 patents. Some of his ideas were odd, and he knew it. He wrote a friend, "If I have a thousand ideas a year, and only one turns out to be good, I'm satisfied."

He still got as many as 50 letters a day. About half of these were requests for money. He turned most of them down. But he did help young people who wished to keep on with their studies. Alfred had his own simple system for filing his mail. He tied the stacks of letters into bundles. He labeled the bundles "Letters from Men," "Letters from Women," and "Begging Letters."

Much can be learned about Alfred Nobel from his answers to these letters. He tried to include some bit of wisdom in each one. Years later a book was published that listed many of his words. Some were:

Lying is the greatest of all sins.
A heart can no more be forced to love than a stomach can be forced to digest food.
Contentment is the only real wealth.

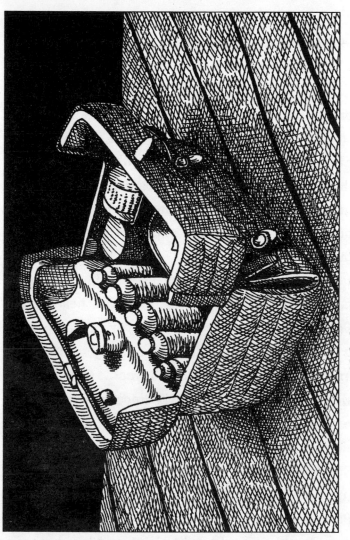

Nobel's traveling bag

Worry is the stomach's worst poison.

Self-respect without the respect of others is
* like a jewel that will not stand the light.*

He called his illnesses *"kind regards from Satan."*

Two things in life that gave Alfred true pleasure were his work in the lab and his thoroughbred horses. In his rare free moments, he could often be found at the race track. His bets on his horses were small. His pleasure in them was great.

He did not like loud noises. The sounds made by carriage wheels gave him a headache. So he invented rubber treads for his carriage wheels. This was an idea that quickly spread. At one point he bought a small yacht. But Alfred was not a sportsman. His health would not permit it.

During his last years, he spent winters at San Remo in Italy. He would travel to Sweden for three months in the summer. He still went to Paris now and then.

By this time both brothers and his mother

had died. Alfred, often kept in bed by illness, was a sad and lonely man. Some nights he could not sleep because of pain. On those nights he spent a lot of time thinking about his will. How could he leave his great wealth so it would benefit the world? How could he show that world what kind of man he really had been? He felt he was not a very good judge of people. He had to make plans so that his fortune would be used to serve the forces of good.

The best days were when he felt strong enough to take the short walk to his lab. November 26, 1896, was just such a day. That afternoon Nobel had a heart attack while working in his lab. Death came quickly. His body was taken home to Sweden.

Chapter 9

The Will

It is not known in what year Alfred Nobel wrote his famous will. He signed it in 1895, a year before his death. It became known as "the will of the dynamite king." Its contents caused much excitement all over the world.

Most of his huge fortune was to be safely and wisely invested. These investments would bring in large sums of money each year. The money would be divided into five parts. It would then be given in the form of prizes to "persons who have rendered the greatest services to mankind." The prizes would go to men and women who worked in:

Physics   Chemistry   Medicine

Literature   Peace

Many people have said that Alfred Nobel himself would have been worthy of receiving two of the prizes – one in Chemistry and one in Peace.

Some of Alfred's nieces and nephews felt overlooked in his will. These were the children of Robert and Ludwig. They were already quite rich. This did not seem to matter to them. They still wanted a piece of this very big "pie." It seemed clear that they were planning to file lawsuits. After many meetings, the matter was settled. Each of the nieces and nephews got a large sum of money. They then promised that they would not sue.

The amount of money each Nobel winner gets is not the same from year to year. How much is given depends on taxes and the interest earned on the investment of Alfred's huge fortune.

The name of each candidate must be submitted in writing by a qualified person. No one is allowed to submit his or her own name. Often men and women will hear that their names have been sent to the Swedish judges. It must be hard for them to wait for the final verdict. They know that if they become a Nobel prize winner, their fame will spread all over the world.

Today the prizes are given in early October. Before that time there is lots of talk in many countries about who the winners will be. The lucky men and women who are chosen must go to Sweden to receive their prizes. They are warmly welcomed there. They often leave Sweden with a great love for that country. Men and women from all over the world have won the Nobel prize.

Four years after Alfred's death, in 1901, the first prizes were presented. They have been given every year since that time. Now and then a prize in one category will not be given. In that case, the prize money is put back into the special fund for that category. Often the prize is shared between two or more people. It is clear that in such cases the judges could not make up their minds as to who was best out of several worthy people.

It is interesting to learn who some of the prize winners have been through the years.

One of the first prize winners in 1901 was William R. Roentgen. He won the Physics prize for his discovery of the X-ray, which has brought so much benefit to the field of medicine.

The famous Italian Guglielmo Marconi won a joint prize in 1909 for his work on the wireless telegraph.

The Nobel prize in Physics in 1966 went to Alfred Kostler of France. He discovered the laser beam.

Life has been greatly improved by winners in Chemistry. We have all heard of Madame Marie Curie of France. She received her Nobel in 1911 for her work in radium.

An Englishman, Frederick Sanger, won the Nobel prize in Chemistry in 1958. He worked on insulin and learned its lifesaving benefits to people with diabetes.

It comes as no surprise that the English

doctor, Sir Alexander Fleming, won the prize in Medicine in 1945. He discovered penicillin. Another miracle drug, streptomycin, of great help in treating tuberculosis, brought a Nobel to an American, Selman Waksman, in 1952.

Many of the discoveries in physics and chemistry that have been won in the late twentieth century would have amazed winners in the early part of the century. They are often given for topics and ideas never heard or dreamed of 75 or 100 years ago.

A lot of names we know can be found in the list of Nobel Literature winners. We see Rudyard Kipling, English; George Bernard Shaw, English; Sinclair Lewis, American; Pearl Buck, American; Sir Winston Churchill, English; Ernest Hemingway, American; John Steinbeck, American. One Russian writer, Boris Pasternak, turned down the prize in 1958. We cannot be sure if that was his own idea. Might it have come from the men who ruled Russia at that time? The men and women who have received Nobel prizes in Literature did not get them for a single book. The award was given for a whole "body of work."

Some famous Peace prize winners have been: Theodore Roosevelt in 1906; Woodrow Wilson in 1920; the International Red Cross in 1917, 1944, and 1963; the United Nations Children's Fund in 1965; Martin Luther King in 1964; Mother Theresa in 1979.

We honor Alfred Nobel because he set a new kind of model for people to admire. Before the Nobel prizes, heroes were men of war, men of wealth, men of high position in business. After the Nobel prizes, such men were replaced. Now the models were men and women who gave up wealth and fame. Alone they searched for knowledge. With others they reached for world peace.

The Nobel award judges do not have a crystal ball. They cannot peer into the future. But the choices they have made to date have stood the test of time. Many of the Nobel awards in Physics, Chemistry, and Medicine have led to a better life for all the world's people.

If we remember the will of the dynamite king which said that the prize should be given to "persons who have rendered the greatest service to mankind," then we can be sure that Alfred Nobel will forever be remembered for his wisdom and his concern for his fellow human beings. He has reached out and touched all of our lives.